VISUAL FOOLERY!

by Michael DiSpezio

FEATURING

Mind benders,

Eye poppers,

Optical illusions,

3-D Images

and
Other Really Weird

but
Vital Stuff

TORMONT

Original Planet Dexter title: *Visual Foolery*
by Michael DiSpezio.
Text copyright © 1995 by the editors of Planet Dexter.
Originally published in the United States
by Addison-Wesley Publishing Company, Inc.

Graphic Design: Zapp

This edition published in 1997 by
Tormont Publications Inc.
338 Saint Antoine St. East
Montreal, Quebec
Canada H2Y 1A3
Tel. (514) 954-1441
Fax (514) 954-5086

ISBN 2-7641-0213-5
Printed in China

Have you ever watched a movie or television show that featured a magician? If so, the magician probably performed some sort of trick. Perhaps a rabbit appeared out of nowhere. Maybe a person was divided in two. In any event, the magician's skill and props led you into seeing something that really didn't happen.

When the trick was over, did you believe in magic? Most likely, not. Instead, you probably thought about what you had seen. Was the table hollow? Could two people fit in the box? Even though you may not have uncovered the magician's secrets, it was fun to be tricked.

Most people like to be fooled. That's why magic is so popular. This book contains other things that can trick you. They're called OPTICAL ILLUSIONS.

By reading this book, you'll learn about all sorts of optical illusions. You'll be tricked by distortions of size, shape and color. Some images will appear as if by magic. Others will seem to disappear! Still others will magically change as you study them.

As you'll soon discover, this book is unlike all other optical illusion books. It not only presents optical illusions, but also explains them. You'll learn about the science of sight. You'll also learn how our brain interprets what our eyes see. But most of all, you'll have fun as you experience the world of optical illusions.

ILLUSIONS

GET READY AND HOLD ON TIGHT!

This book is your ticket to a fantastic journey through the world of illusions.

As you'll discover, its pages are packed full of optical illusions, neat facts, exciting adventures and fun projects.

Are you ready to begin?

GOOD

See the ticket at the right?

Are the red and blue lines the same length, or is one line longer than the other?

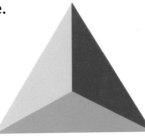

ADMIT ONE

Although they may not look it, the red and blue lines are exactly the same length. The shape of this ticket fools your brain into seeing something that appears different from what it actually is. That's called an **ILLUSION**.

NOW TAKE A LOOK BELOW.

Close your right eye and look at this triangle.

Slowly bring your eye closer to the book.

WHAT HAPPENS TO THE STAR?

At a certain distance the star disappears. This type of illusion occurs because the star's image falls on a part of your eye that is not sensitive to light.

Examine the picture of the eye on the next page. Can you figure out which part of the eye causes the star to disappear?

AND THE EYE

The *iris* is a muscular disk that expands and contracts to control the size of the pupil. Your eye color is the color of the iris.

The *lens* is a clear muscle. By changing shape, it helps focus light on the back of the eye.

This clear, outer covering is called the *cornea.* It protects your eye.

This black spot is a hole through which light passes to get inside the eye. This opening is called the *pupil.*

The *blind* spot is found where the optic nerve joins the retina. In this area, we have no light-sensitive cells.

The *optic nerve* is a bundle of nerve fibers that moves messages from the eye to the brain and back.

The *retina* is the layer that lines the back and sides of the inner eye. It contains light-sensitive cells called rods and cones. To learn more about these cells, turn to page 30.

The *cones* are cells that produce images in color.

The *rods* are cells that produce images with shades of gray.

Eye Opener

Did you know that most babies are born with blue eyes? The pigments that produce darker eyes may take months to form.

Mind Messages

The rods and cones of our retinas produce nerve messages. These messages travel along the optic nerve. As the messages move, they are sorted. Some messages carry information about movement; other messages carry information about appearance. Our brain combines these messages, using them to construct a complete view of what we see.

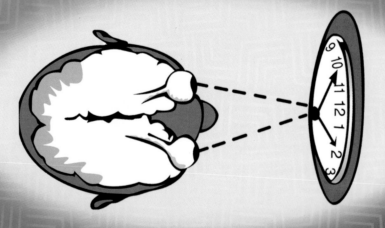

Sometimes our brain receives clashing messages. When the brain's messages clash, illusions can be produced.

TRY THIS:

ROLL A SHEET OF PAPER INTO A TUBE.

Now hold the tube next to your hand as shown here. With both eyes open, look through the tube AND at your hand.

What do you see?

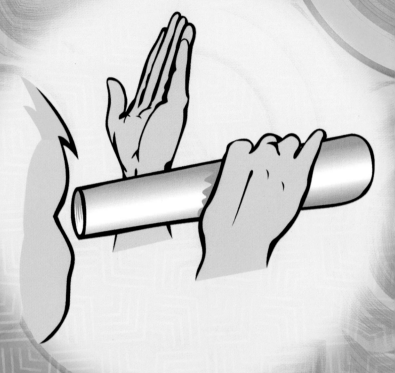

One eye detects a hand. The other eye sees through the tube.

For much of your life, your brain has combined the images from both eyes. Most of the time, the combination produces a wideview. This time, however, it produces an OPTICAL ILLUSION.

DELIGHTS

Take a look at the painting below.

Is there anything strange about the *Mona Lisa's* appearance
(*other than being upside down*)?

Think about it.

Then flip this page

upside down...

...upside down....

Leonardo da Vinci, *Mona Lisa*
Musée du Louvre, Paris

Her eyes and mouth are turned over! When you first looked at the upside-down portrait, your brain became confused about what was up and what wasn't. It was so stumped that you didn't notice that the eyes and mouth weren't flipped over. When you looked at the painting right-side up, however, the confusion was gone. Your brain quickly spotted the face parts that weren't right.

DISTORTIONS

Which vertical (up and down) line is longer?

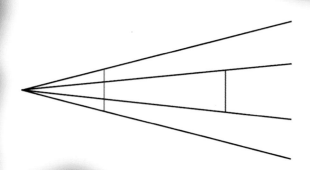

(After you make your guess, you may want to use a ruler to compare actual lengths.)

As you may have guessed (but didn't observe), the lines are the same length. The illusion to the left is an example of size distortion. Size distortions occur when images or backgrounds incorrectly remind us of similar things.

Which line below appears longer,

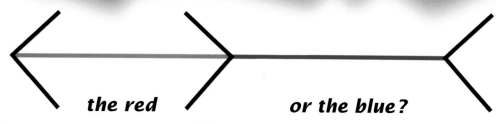

the red   or the blue?

Muller-Lyer Illusion

To most people, the blue line will appear longer.

Here's why:

The first set of lines looks like the edge of a building. In the real world, this leading edge appears taller. Our brain, however, has learned that all corners of the building are the same height. Knowing this, our brain does an automatic "shrinking adjustment" to cut the line down to size.

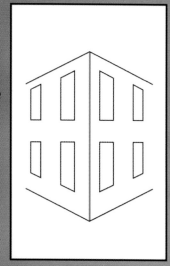

Likewise, the other set of lines looks like the distant corner of a room. Because the room height must be uniform, our brain does an automatic "enlarging adjustment". The results mislead us about the lines' lengths.

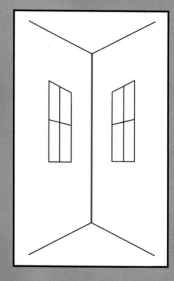

DISTORTIONS

Distortions can be produced in many other ways.
Which lines below are the same length?

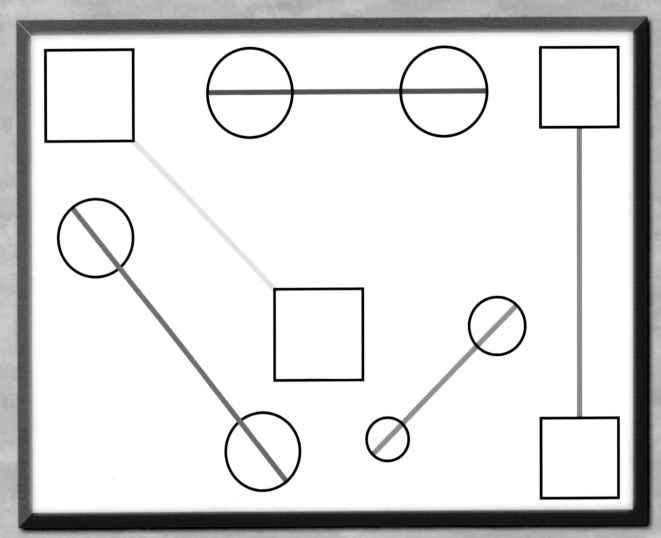

The red and blue lines are the same length.
So are the green and yellow lines.

When we enclose a line, the line appears shorter.

LOOK BELOW ▲

Which flower pattern contains the larger black circle?

Both black circles are the same size. The surrounding circles caused this illusion. Your brain compared the size of the surrounding circles to the inner circles. When the inner circle was surrounded by smaller circles, it made sense to think of this black circle as *large*. When the inner circle was surrounded by larger circles, it made sense to consider it a *small* circle.

Ebbinghaus' Illusion

Will the box on the left fit into the space between the two boxes on the right?

(It might not look like it, but the white box on the left and the black area on the right are the same size.)

White or brightly colored objects reflect light, so bright light striking the retina can "bleed" outward. This effect causes neighboring cells to detect the image, making it seem larger.

When the object is dark or black, its image does not "bleed" outward. Neighboring cells are not affected, so the image does not look bigger than it really is.

TALL and WIDE

Another length illusion is based on the estimation of

HEIGHT
and
WIDTH

Are these "T"s as tall as they are wide?

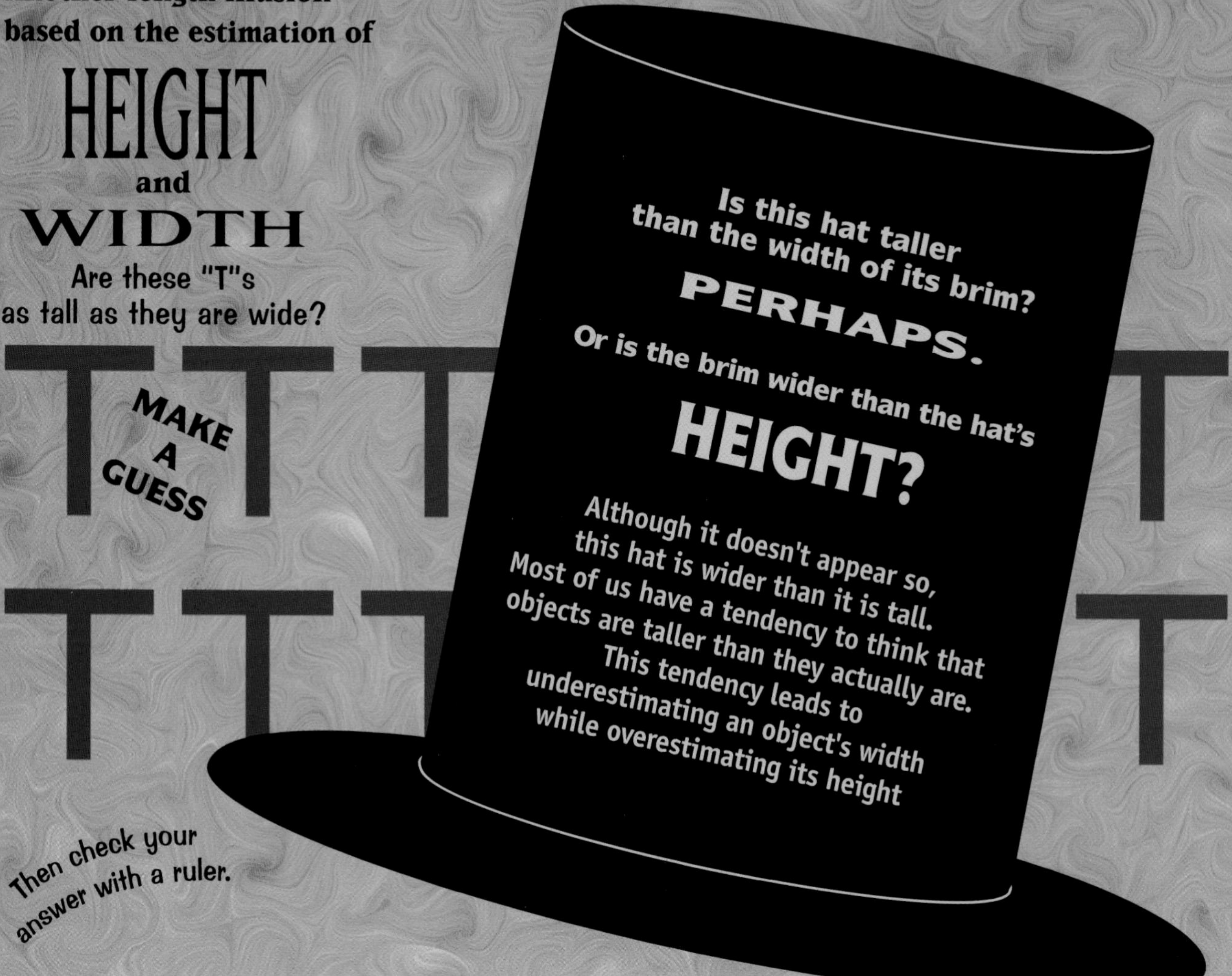

T T T T T T

MAKE A GUESS

Then check your answer with a ruler.

Is this hat taller than the width of its brim?

PERHAPS.

Or is the brim wider than the hat's

HEIGHT?

Although it doesn't appear so, this hat is wider than it is tall. Most of us have a tendency to think that objects are taller than they actually are. This tendency leads to underestimating an object's width while overestimating its height

Look at the triangle at the right.

IS THE DOT CLOSER TO THE TOP OR THE BOTTOM, OR IS IT EQUIDISTANT?

Like the hat, the figure at the left is a perfect example of this illusion. The dot is equidistant. When we look at it, however, we overestimate its height.

BENDS AND TILTS

Many distortions include two images, a foreground figure and a background pattern.

Take a look at the triangle and pattern of circles below. When placed over a field of circles, however, the triangle's sides appear to bend inward.

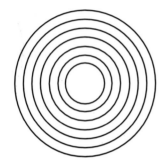 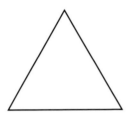 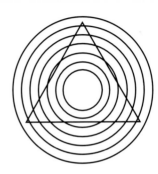

Here are some other shape illusions.
All are produced by the background pattern.

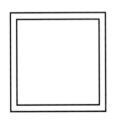 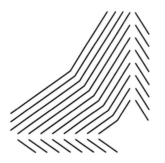 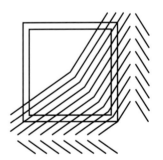

Patterns can also make straight objects appear tilted or change a line's path. Sometimes the pattern is in the background. Other times, an object is filled with a pattern. Still other times, the pattern makes up the object's outline.

Take a look at the word "TILT" below.

Are the letters tilted?

To double-check, examine this page from a distance.

TILT

AMAZED?

It's the jagged outline pattern that makes the letters appear slanted.

Can you believe TILT isn't tilted?

OOK AT THE PATTERN BELOW.

Do the vertical (up and down) columns look straight, or are they tilted?

You may want to use a straight edge to double-check your answer.

BENDS AND TILTS

Here are some other examples of tilting, slanting and misaligned lines!

Does line A meet up with line B or C?
Use a ruler to find out.

WEIRD, HUH?

A

B C

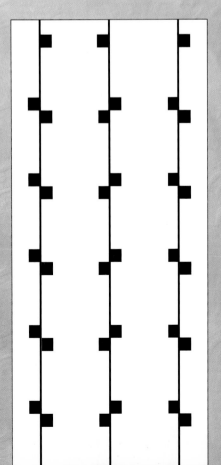

Do the lines to the left tilt toward each other or away from each other?

NEITHER!

The little boxes make them look tilted, but they're not.

CLOSURE

Illusory figures can also have three-dimensional appearance. Often, these illusions resemble high-contrast photographs. Because the images are not complete, your mind must tie together the separate parts. This is called *closure*.

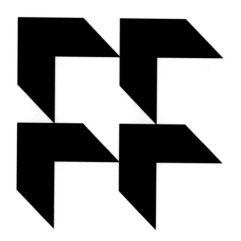

Look at the pattern to the left.

Can you see the four black arrowheads pointing to the top left corner?

GooD

Now can you see the four cubes stacked next to each other?

The three-dimensional appearance of the cubes results from closure.

Now take a look at the images below.

Can you figure out what each object is?
If you can't, don't worry.
The names of the objects are spelled out at the bottom of this page.

ILLUSORY FIGURES

Can you see the white triangle in the figure below?
It probably appears a little whiter than the rest of the page.

SEE IT? GREAT!

The only problem is that the triangle you see doesn't exist!

Your mind has constructed an imaginary triangle from the broken lines and cut-out pie shapes. This type of illusion is called an *illusory figure*.

Illusory figures are a result of "thinking shortcuts". These shortcuts allow us to quickly make sense of what we see without having to examine the entire appearance of an object.

Illusory figures are powerful illusions that can be made to appear with very few lines and shapes. Even when the cut-outs are replaced by dots, a white triangle appears.

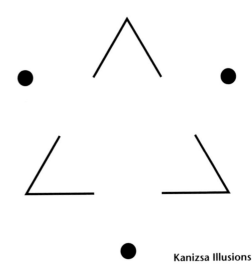

Kanizsa Illusions

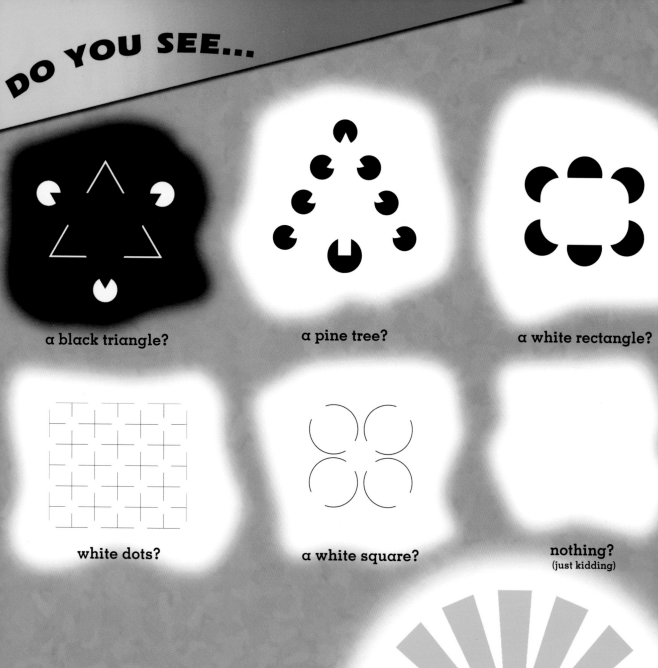

a black triangle?

a pine tree?

a white rectangle?

white dots?

a white square?

nothing?
(just kidding)

Lines that appear to fade away can produce illusory figures.

Can you see a sunlike object at the center of these lines?

UNSTABLE FIGURES

Some illusions, however, aren't nearly as permanent as the ones on pages 18 and 19. As you view them, their appearance flip-flops. These illusions are called unstable figures.

Unstable figures alternate between two or more appearances. Each appearance makes as much sense as the other. Because our brain can't decide which one works best, the image takes on an unstable identity.

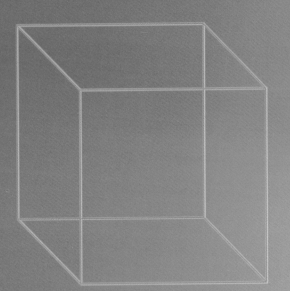

Take a look at the box on the left. Can you see the two appearances of this cube?

For some people, both views are obvious.
For others, finding both images is just not that easy.

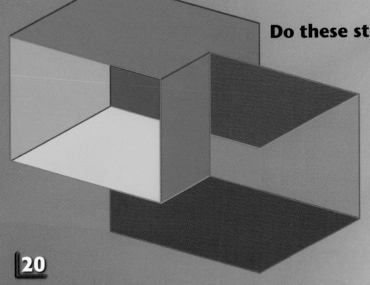

Do these strange boxes open from the right...

or from the left...

or from both directions?

Take a look at these unstable figures.

Can you see both appearances?

If not, try turning the page upside down.

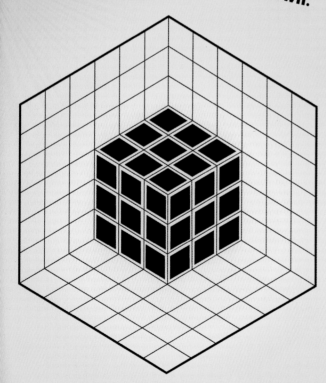

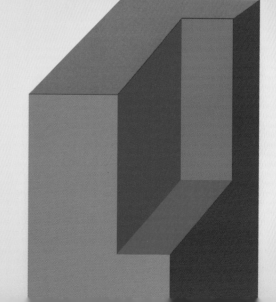

FLATS AND FACES

Images sometimes "pop" from a two-dimensional drawing to what appears to be an object with three dimensions. The brick box on the right looks three-dimensional (3-D). Artists sometimes produce three-dimensional cues so well that it's hard to see the flat drawing from which the image came.

Some patterns make great unstable figures!

Turn the boxes upside down.

How many do you see now?

IMPOSSIBLE FIGURES

Have you ever put together something that was impossible to build?

Really, really impossible?

Have you built something as impossible as this illustration?

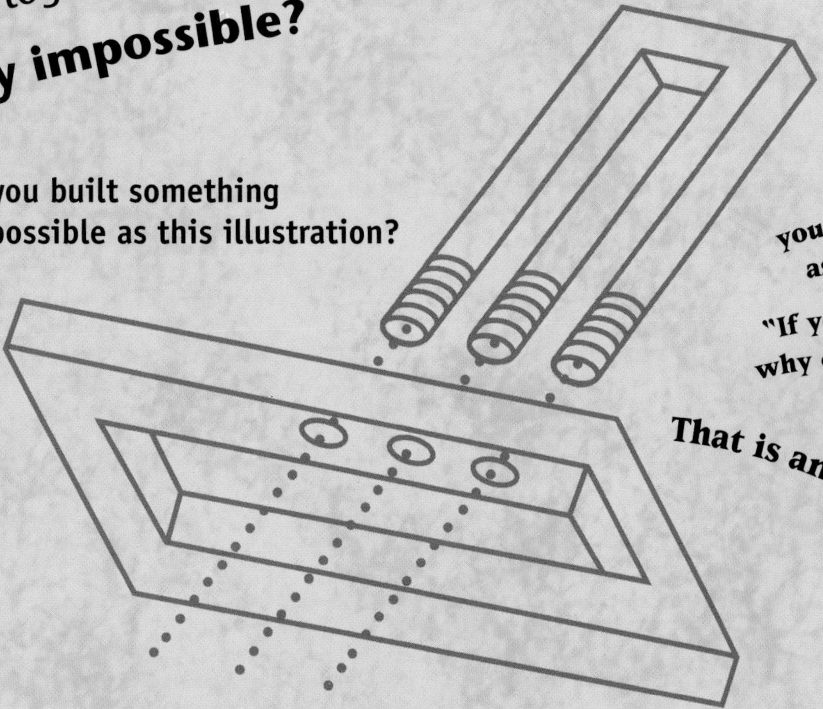

Right now, you are probably asking yourself,

"If you can draw it, why can't you build it?"

That is an excellent question.

Most likely, you have not, because this really is an impossible figure. Although it can be drawn, an object like this can't be built.

Because the drawing is flat, things can be drawn in any way. In other words, you can cheat. When you try to use these drawings as blueprints, however, you run into difficulties.

You see, impossible figures are unstable. Just look at the illustration on the right, and you'll see that parts of the drawing look right. But if you look at all the parts at once, the image becomes unstable.

Eye Opener

The number of boards you see in this stack depends on the side from which you look. When you try to see both sides of the stack together, the image becomes a flip-flopping illusory figure.

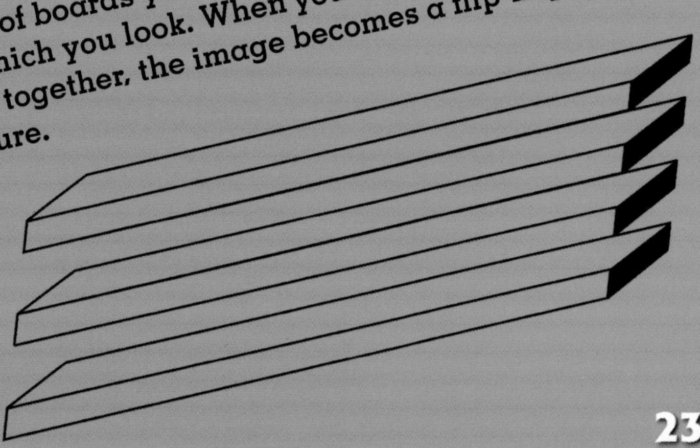

Take a look at this castle's staircase.

TAKE A GOOD LOOK.

Notice anything unusual?

Turn to the last page to find the illusion that is the basis of this drawing.

**The Dutch artist M.C. Escher
drew this strange scene.
He based many of his drawings
on impossible and unstable figures.**

Do you think you can also draw a scene based on an illusion?
Which illusion would you select?

d'impossible

Here's another impossible scene.

This one was painted by Belgian-born artist René Magritte.

René Magritte, "The Blank Signature" 1965 © 1997 C. Herscovici, Brussels/Artists Rights Society (ARS), New York
Photograph © 1997 The National Gallery of Art, Washington, D.C.

25

IMAGE STRETCH

Have you ever written a secret message? If so, what type of code did you use?

Take a look at the pattern of lines shown to the left.

Can you guess how to decode this message?

This is an example of a stretched image illusion. When the figure is "unstretched", the hidden image appears.

To unstretch this image, hold the bottom edge of the book up to your eye. Look across the pag and the message will appear.

Eye Opener

Safety signs painted onto roadways are sometimes stretched out. Why do you think these messages are distorted in this way?

LOOK FROM HERE

Take a look at the photos to the right. They were all stretched by computer.

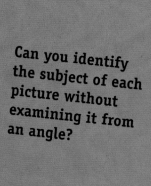

Can you identify the subject of each picture without examining it from an angle?

MIRROR GAMES

Funhouse mirrors can distort your appearance. Their curved surfaces stretch and squish your reflection. But did you know that the reverse is also true? A distorted image can be corrected by a curved mirror.

More than one hundred years ago, special toy viewers appeared. These viewers were small cylinders that had mirrored surfaces. When placed on a stretched picture, the viewer corrected the distorted image.

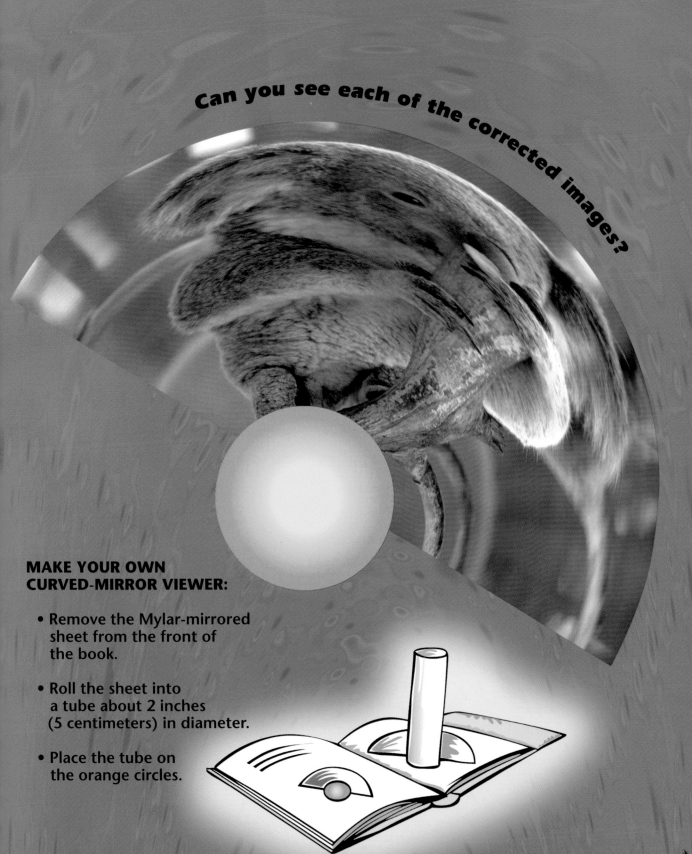

Can you see each of the corrected images?

MAKE YOUR OWN CURVED-MIRROR VIEWER:

- Remove the Mylar-mirrored sheet from the front of the book.

- Roll the sheet into a tube about 2 inches (5 centimeters) in diameter.

- Place the tube on the orange circles.

COLORS AND SHADES

How many different colors do you see?

NOW DIM THE LIGHTS.

How many different colors are there?

The eye's retina contains two types of cells that react to light: **rods** and **cones** *(see page 5 for a picture)*. When struck by light, these cells produce messages that travel to the brain.

Rods can detect tiny amounts of light. These cells allow us to see in dim light. Rods transform colors into shades of gray.

Cones react only to bright light. They do not detect dark or dim things. Unlike rods, cones produce our color vision.

Now turn back to the illusion above. In bright light, your cones identified each color. In dim light, your cones didn't work. Instead it was your rods that reacted. Because rods cannot distinguish colors, all of the blocks appeared to be a similar shade of gray.

How many shades of orange fill the block below?

NOW DIVIDE THE BLOCK IN HALF WITH YOUR FINGER.

How many shades are there?

The shade of color we see depends on its contrast to the surrounding background.

When you divided the block, the darker background produced a lighter orange shade. Likewise, the lighter background produced the appearance of a darker orange.

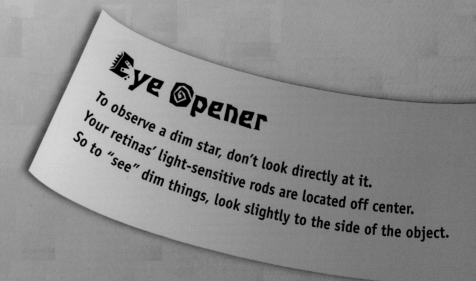

Eye Opener

To observe a dim star, don't look directly at it. Your retinas' light-sensitive rods are located off center. So to "see" dim things, look slightly to the side of the object.

AFTER IMAGES

Stare at the center of the bull's-eye for about 10 seconds.

Try not to blink or move.

Then switch your focus to the star.

The image that appears at the star is called an *afterimage*.
How is the afterimage illusion like the original image?

How is it different?

Afterimages appear after our vision has been
overstimulated. Staring for a long time at a picture or bright lights
can cause overstimulation, which will temporarily "imprint" an image on
your eye. When you look away from the image, you'll still see a fleeting copy
of what you were looking at, but in opposite colors *(sort of like a
photographic negative)*.

Stare at the dot in the center of the image on the left for about 15 seconds.

Then switch your focus to the star located in the center of the image on the right.

DAILY SUN

KING SEEN EVERYWHERE

Stare at the star in the center of the blue lines for about 20 seconds.

Then shift your focus to the dot in the middle of the white cat.

WHAT HAPPENS?

Wandering Eyes

Have you ever felt that someone was watching you?

Here's your chance to build a mad dog that won't take its eyes off you. Take out the mad dog page included in the front pocket of the book.

1 Cut out the eye slip.

2 Cut out the two eye holes and the two slits.

3 Insert tab A into slit A, and insert tab B into slit B. Tape into place.

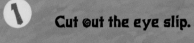

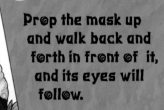

4 Prop the mask up and walk back and forth in front of it, and its eyes will follow.

Scary, huh?

Because the eyes and the face are at different distances, they appear to move at different speeds. The face *(with its cut-out eye openings)* moves faster. The distant eyes move more slowly. As you walk, these different speeds create a "shifty" pair of watchful eyes.

MOTION MAGIC

Watch a spinning spiral, and your eye can't help but be drawn to its center! Then look away from the spiral.

- Take the spiral disk pattern from the front pocket of the book.
- Push a tack through the center of the disk.
- Then push the tack into the end of a pencil's eraser.
- Make sure that the tack does not bind the disk too tightly. The disk should spin freely, but not wobble.

BIG FACES

- Spin the disk so that the spiral appears to be "going in".
- Keep spinning at a constant speed for about 20 seconds.
- Keep your focus at the center of the disk. Then focus on someone's face.

What happens to the face?

LITTLE FACES

- Repeat the same activity.
- This time, however, spin the disk so that the spiral appears to be expanding.
- After about 20 seconds, focus on someone's face.

EVERYTHING APPEARS TO GET LARGER!

What happens now?

3-D

Before reading this page, remove the red-and-blue glasses from the side of the book.

THEN PUT THE GLASSES ON AND EXPERIENCE
THE EFFECT AS YOU LEARN ABOUT IT!

This 3-D effect can only be seen using colored viewing glasses. The stereoprint (*red and blue 3-D art*) is made of a right-eye view and a left-eye view.

One view is red.

The other is blue.

The colored views are printed right on top of each other.

To make sense of this jumble, you need to use special red-and-blue glasses. The red lens allows only the blue image to reach its eye. Likewise, the blue lens only allows the red image to reach the other eye.

The result is a separated view that you see as 3-D!

Bryce O'Lanterns

© 1994 Saint

© 1994 Harry St. Ours

MORE 3-D

© 1996 Photo manipulation by Hal Morgan

Stereograms

Another type of 3-D illusion is produced using patterns of dots; it's called a *stereogram*. Like other binocular illusions, this one is also based on seeing two side-by-side views. (*See page 42 for a definition of "binocular vision".*) The views, however, are hidden in a jumble of dots.

When your brain puts the two images together, a new 3-D form "pops" out of the picture.

● ●

A chameleon.

To see these 3-D figures try the following techniques:

- Hold the image about a foot away (30 centimeters), and look into the dots. Relax and let your eyes drift. Don't try to focus on the dots; look "through" the dots instead. The image should appear.

- Begin with the image touching your nose. Slowly move the image back, but don't try to focus. Keep the image about a foot (30 centimeters) away, and relax your eyes. The image should appear.

- Look at the two focusing dots at the top of the picture. Let your eyes drift so that the two dots become one. Once that happens, look down, and the image should appear.

A dinosaur.

TWO-EYED TRICKS

Two eyes are better than one.

Not only do two eyes give a wider view, but they also work together to help us know how close or far things are from us. This is called **DEPTH PERCEPTION.**

TRY THIS

- Look at a distant object.
- Now hold up a finger at arm's length.
- Close one eye and observe the position of the finger against the background object.
- Now switch eyes.

What happens to the finger?

The finger appears to jump!
Now hold the finger a few inches
(about 5 centimeters) from your nose.
Look at the same object and alternate eyes.

What happens now?

When your finger is closer, it seems to jump a greater distance. When it's farther away, it seems to jump less. The "jumping" is caused by viewing the same object from two separate eyes.

This type of seeing is called *binocular vision.*

Did you know that your brain uses one of your eyes more than the other? It's called your *dominant* eye, and it's the view from this eye that you rely on most.

To tell if you are left-eyed or right-eyed, hold up a finger and look at a distant object. Close one eye. Then open it. Does the finger shift position? Now close the other eye. Then open it. Does the finger shift position now? The non-shifting view was seen through your dominant eye.

Is your right or left eye dominant?

NOW TRY THIS TWO-EYED TRICK.

• Make a floating finger hot dog by holding your hands about a foot (30 centimeters) away from your face.

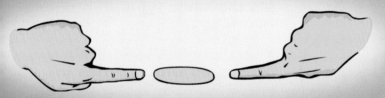

Look at this "X" from the bottom edge of the book. Do you see the extra line? This line is caused by the crossing over of each eye's vision.

• Stare past your fingers, and slowly touch the tips of your index fingers (see illustration above). As you pull your fingers apart, what happens?

Eye Opener

Ever wonder why you're not aware of your blind spot? (See page 5 for the definition of "blind spot".) Part of the reason is that the blind spot of one eye doesn't align with the blind spot of the other. So each eye supplies the other eye's missing vision. Another reason is that our brain fills in the missing spots with what it thinks should be there.

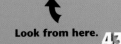

Look from here.

FLIP BOOK

Hey, kid! Want to make a movie?

Remove the "flip book" from the side of the book.

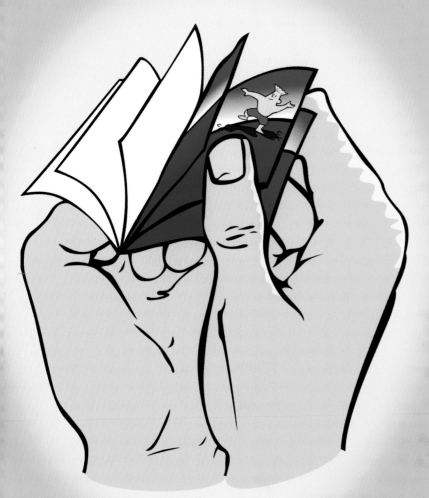

As you flip through the images, they'll look as though they're moving. The motion you see is an illusion. In fact, it's the same type of illusion that makes movies and videos possible. When our brain is presented with a series of changing pictures, it tries to sort them out. If the images are presented slowly, we see them as separate and distinct. If, however, the images change too quickly, our brain can't keep up. Instead, we "see" what appears to be smooth motion.

PENCIL FLIPPER

A pencil flipper uses just two images to produce motion.

To build a flipper:

- Remove the two-frame motion card from the front pocket of the book.

- Bend the card along the dotted line.

- Staple the ends together.

- Slip the frames over the end of a pencil and secure with tape.

- Snap your hands back and forth, making the frames alternate positions.

Does the bat take flight?

Kinematoscope

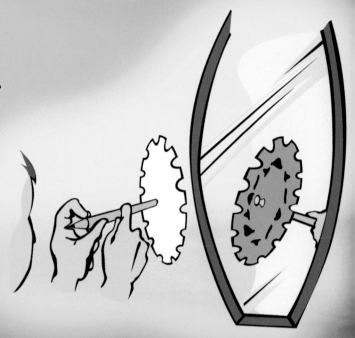

Like a flip book, a kinematoscope produces the illusion of smooth motion. This device first appeared in the 1880s. It was inexpensive and easy to build. It was also fun! The only problem was that the movie lasted less than a second.

To build your own kinematoscope:

- Remove the frame disk from the front pocket of the book.

- Push a tack through the center of the disk and secure it to the eraser end of a pencil.

- Make sure that the disk rotates freely.

- Stand in front of a mirror and spin the disk.

As you peer through the moving slots, you'll observe an incredible reflection!

As you have learned, the illusion of motion is produced when things appear too fast to be sorted.

Our brain can also get confused when trying to follow odd shapes.

WEIRD LOOP

To build the spinner:

- Remove the weird loop disk from the front pocket of the book.

- Assemble a kinematoscope-like spinner.

- Slowly rotate the disk.
(You don't need to use the mirror this time.)

What happens to the shape?

Does the illusion change with speed?

MISSION COMPLETED

That's just about it for this Visual Adventure. It's been a journey that's taken you from how things are to how things aren't always what they seem. From now on, keep your eyes and mind open, and you'll find illusions all around you.

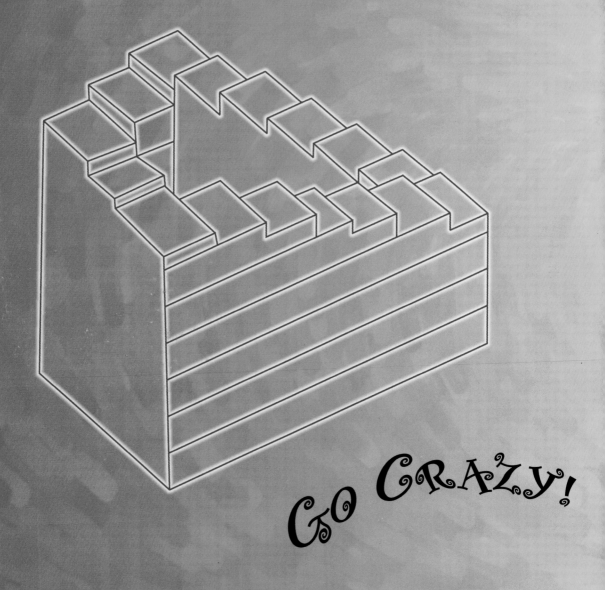

Go CRAZY!